On Motherhood

Published by: Amanda J. Smith and Katie Hetman

ISBN: 9798845849908

Front image by OpenClipart-Vectors from Pixabay, silhouette art by Mohamed Hassan from Pixabay.

To our five children: May you always feel the strength that you have given us.

It was 1 a.m. and she was 38 weeks pregnant. A small cramp woke her from sleep, and she wondered, is this what the beginning of labor feels like? Throughout her pregnancy journey she asked herself that question time and time again. Would she be able to handle the pain, the drive to the hospital? Would they make it in time?

Her doula thought perhaps it was Braxton Hicks since the cramping wasn't too severe. She went to work the next morning, and the cramping worsened. Still, she wondered, is this what labor feels like?

She stood at work in gown and gloves, sweating from head to toe. She realized, this is what labor feels like. The pain went from harsh cramps to something more. The experience grew, her senses heightened…she knew, her life was inches from incredible change.

We love talking to mothers and mothers-to-be

about their pregnancy, delivery, adoption or surrogacy journey because the experience varies so widely, and there's an unspoken bond that forms in the process. That's what makes it a little scary beforehand, you never really know what your story will be. But there is a magic in that, too.

For some, pregnancy and motherhood books can be daunting, or the morning sickness too severe to read long pieces of text. Some books have a perspective that doesn't match their own, or the subject matter doesn't quite fit. Because of this, we realized that a nonjudgmental book was needed, not from the opinions of one, but from the perspectives of many.

In your hand is a guide: handfuls of wisdom from mothers interviewed around the world. Take comfort in knowing that you're not alone in the journey, and regardless of country or age, there are similarities in the love, challenges and known misconceptions. We hope you open

these pages and feel a togetherness that we felt
when writing it.

Chapter 1

On What You'll Love Most

Kindness and Grace

We brought home our sweet baby, the day our family grew.

Life has changed so much. Am I the girl you still once knew?

You send me a wink as we scramble through the day.

A kiss on the cheek as we pass in the hallway.

Thankful every morning for your smiling face.

Amazed with how you parent with your kindness and your grace.

I was worried how we would change, would the flame die?

But you're the wind under my wing and with you I fly.

The strongest team together still in love, forever and longer.

Our bundle of joy is a blessing and has made us even stronger.

-Katie Hetman

"There is absolutely nothing in the world like watching this little person that you helped create learn how to walk and talk and think for themselves. I absolutely love seeing my son's creative side come out and watching his imagination go a mile a minute and to think that I was there for all of those steps. It really is true what they say about a piece of your heart walking around outside of your body."

-Amy, North Carolina, USA

"The pride you get from watching your child grow and become their own individual. Every day they learn something new and it's just amazing to watch them grow and develop."

-Kate, New Jersey, USA

"Finding out there's a whole other part of your being that you didn't even know existed. You get introduced to the version of you that would do literally ANYTHING to protect your child, and you'll FINALLY understand (in full) your own mother/father's love for you."

-Jamie, Colorado, USA

"Watching your children grow is so amazing. It is so rewarding- It is bittersweet. Sweet watching them grow and learn, but bitter because time flies. Never miss times with your children. Other things can wait. It's time you will never get back."

-Destany, Colorado, USA

"How do you answer that? That first time you hold them… there is nothing quite like that."

-Anne, Colorado, USA

"Whatever you love will be unique to you and it will be a discovery! You get to keep growing that love and discovering that love. You get to keep loving more."

-Dylan, North Carolina, USA

"I loved breastfeeding. I loved that I was the one to bring comfort and peace to my baby."

-Anonymous, New Mexico, USA

"Having a little human that loves you
more than anything."

-Kelly, Massachusetts, USA

"The strength it gives you!!! Being a mom unlocks some superpower inside you. You have instincts, intuitions, and speed you never knew you had. You also realize that you can do amazing things with literally zero sleep."

-Kara, New Mexico, USA

"The uniqueness! Every time a baby is born there's a very unique story to tell."

-Nicole, Manchester, UK

"Unconditional Love."

-Lauren, Colorado, USA

"Having a little person to take care of who loves you unconditionally. You will mature and grow in ways to be an independent woman who a baby is dependent on."

-Georgia, Surrey, UK

"For me, breastfeeding felt powerful. To know I am nourishing that perfect thing in a perfect way gave me bigger pride than earning my Ph.D. Motherhood is also harder than a Ph.D."

-Emma, California, USA

"There is so much to love about motherhood. After the birth of my first child, I was in awe at how quickly my perspective on the world shifted. I had so much more empathy and love for others. I stopped seeing people (for the most part) as the jerk who cut me off in traffic or the annoying lady taking forever in front of me at the checkout line. Instead, I started seeing everyone as someone else's child.

When I'd get angry or annoyed with someone, I would remember, that is someone's child. Someone loves that person more than anything in the world, just like I love this little boy more than anything. The second time, I was surprised by what our hearts are capable of again, but in a different way. This may sound strange, but I feared I wouldn't be able to love my second child because my heart was SO FULL with love for my firstborn. How could I make room for her when he was already taking up all the space in my heart? It turns out, we don't make room for the next child. Our heart grows and makes new space."

-Marisa, Illinois, USA

"Snuggles. It doesn't matter what age, snuggles, and squeezes from tiny people are all you need. The warmth of their sleeping bodies is like a sleeping potion, the squeeze from their tiny arms are all the purpose you need."

-Melissa, California, USA

"The smell of Johnson's baby shampoo in your baby's hair. The sweet snuggles as you nurse and they face you with complete adoration. The fact that you could never love anyone as much as you love this little baby."

-Jennie, Arizona, USA

"For me, it fulfilled a calling I've known in my heart all my life. I guess that doesn't apply to everyone, but that's how I feel!"

-Molly, Colorado, USA

"The sweet moments of unconditional love you feel for and from your child. There's nothing like it and worth every sleepless night, worry, and heartache."

-Tiffany, Washington, USA

Chapter 2

On Pregnancy and Delivery

Today I'll Be a Mom

Did I just pee my pants? Or did my water just

break?

They said I would know. Is all this advice fake?

Am I in labor now? I think I felt a contraction.

This has to be it! Hunny, are you ready for action?

Get the bag, the car seat I think it's time to go.

Wait, maybe not, everything is starting to slow.

I can't sleep am I nervous? Nope just super

nauseous.

Should we go to the hospital just to be cautious?

I sit on a ball with a timer. Was it five-one-one?

Yes! I'm in labor! Hurry we need to run.

My mind racing. Trying to keep myself calm.

Scared but so excited! Today I'll be a mom.

-Katie Hetman

"...Take it all in, mama. And know that our bodies are amazing creatures, capable of things you could never hear from any story."
-Anne, Colorado, USA

"Being that we are a family by adoption, my advice comes from what I watched our son's birth mother go through. Whether it is your first or fifth pregnancy, I think it's crucial to know how badass your body is. You are seriously doing something (i.e. growing a human) that will change the world. You are giving your body for the greater good and all the changes that occur, whether physically, mentally, emotionally, or spiritually are proof of the selfless love you have for your child."

-Kate, New Jersey, USA

"Take it as it comes. It won't all be smooth, and it won't be how you planned it, but when you look back it will still be special."
-Melanie, UK

"Always do what feels right for YOU and don't feel pressured to do anything otherwise. It's nice to have a 'plan' in place to help you feel prepared but make sure to also be open to changes, especially last minute. I really think that helped me enjoy my pregnancies and births. I had an end goal of getting my babies here safely, I had things I wanted to happen a certain way, but I was flexible if those things needed to change to keep me and the baby safe."

-Jamie, Colorado, USA

"My advice on pregnancy (since it took us 7 IVF rounds to have our 2 daughters), is to never say never. A friend of ours who did IVF as well as international adoption gave us this advice and it served us well. Infertility is full of ups and downs and it's easy to start out thinking, I'll try IUI but never IVF, or I'll do IVF but never (insert here). It's good to keep an open mind when it comes to many things but most certainly the crazy world of infertility."

-Lauren, Colorado, USA

"My advice on pregnancy, delivery, and beyond is to go with the flow. This is such a hard thing to do but so important. Everyone has an idea in their head of how they want their pregnancy and delivery to go, and in some cases, things will go exactly as you hope. However, the majority of the time there are factors outside of your control and you have to let go of your expectations and allow your story to take on its own narrative. Though your story and your experience may not be what you expected, try to find the beauty in the story that is yours."

-Amy, North Carolina, USA

"I really enjoyed being pregnant. It's such a special time and I feel like I got so many extra kind smiles and gestures when I was pregnant. I often thought why that was, but I believe people truly think growing a child is a beautiful and wonderful thing. A mom gets the unique opportunity to get to know her little one in utero and how they move and interact with their world. My advice would be to start learning to embrace how your body changes to accommodate a new life! All of the new curves and soft spots and giant thighs are for the very special purpose of making your baby! And just as life is forever changed with a baby, so is your body, and that's not a bad thing! It is a reminder of how amazing you are to have created a life inside you."

-Kara, New Mexico, USA

"Accept the unexpected …. Everyone's story is different and no matter how much you plan you never know what could happen. A whole human being is coming out of your body, things may not go as planned."
-Anonymous, New Mexico, USA

"Enjoy every minute and do what feels right!
Don't worry about changing the plan 100 times,
have a flexible mindset, whatever happens,
happens for a reason."

-Nicole, UK

"Go with the flow and trust your body. Don't be afraid of changes that have to be made during labor. You are stronger than you think and are capable of giving birth."
-Georgia, Surrey, England

"As with everything related to parenting, you have to do what feels right for you, and sometimes it's painful or scary or weird, but carrying and delivering (however you go about it) is the coolest thing you will ever do. Ever."

-Marisa, Illinois, USA

"Get a doula! It's great to have an advocate and resource on all things related to pregnancy."

-Anonymous

"During both my pregnancies my husband has been beyond helpful and supportive…He has taken care of our toddler and made me dinner when I've had terrible morning sickness, he has done 90% of the dishes. He has rubbed my back, comforted me, gotten up for night feeds, he has done it all. As a fiercely independent person, this was all very uncomfortable for me in the beginning as I imagine it would be for most women. Moms, I'd encourage you to consider this: it is a small blip in the life of your marriage. Be thankful, be gracious, accept the help, and know there are so many years ahead to show the same kindness."

-Melissa, California, USA

"For me, there was a beauty in the pain. But no matter how you deliver: non-medicated, c-section, epidural…you've given birth. The child came out of you, and no matter what that looks like, it's simply amazing… and it's because of you. If you have lingering guilt or sadness from some part of the labor or pregnancy process, just know you did the best you could under the most pain of your life, and you're amazing for it. Believe it."

-Anonymous, New Mexico, USA

"It can be scary carrying a child after a loss, however that may have looked. It's often not talked about, but know that many of us understand, and you're not alone in the utter love you feel, but also how scary it can be in the ultrasound room, or even at delivery. Just remember, you are strong mama, and others understand."

-Anonymous

"Expect the unexpected. No amount of prepping or reading will prepare you for what experience itself will teach you."

-Tiffany, Washington, USA

"Taking care of yourself at this stage is what a mother does to take care of her unborn child."

-Nat, Canada

Chapter 3

On Mental Health

Pandemic Pregnancy

I carry your life and hope but I'm surrounded by despair.

I stay home, cover my face, because it wouldn't be fair.

I want to give you the best chance to grow and live a life healthy and long.

But I distance myself, isolated, lonely, but strong.

Missed weddings and funerals to keep you safe little one.

Not living in fear but making you a priority my son.

I know I can't protect you from all the dangers I fear.

But I promise to do my best to keep you safe until you are here.

-Katie Hetman

"Taking care of yourself is JUST as important as taking care of your children. If you aren't ok, ask for help. There are so many changes that happen mentally and physically that it's normal to be overwhelmed, but what isn't normal is feeling sad or anxious 24/7. Even though it's not normal, it's very common and affects the majority of Mothers in varying degrees. You haven't done anything wrong, by asking for help you are doing everything right! I suffered from Severe Post-Partum Anxiety with both my children. With the medical and therapeutic interventions, I received I was able to find 'Me' again and enjoy early motherhood."

-Tiffany, Washington, USA

"You are not going crazy! Even if you don't give birth, post-adoption depression and anxiety are very real! You are not a failure if you don't feel like you are connecting to your child. Getting counseling or medication does not mean you aren't a wonderful mom. If you don't fill your own cup, there is no way you can take care of your new baby. I think it's important to also know that your partner may get postpartum depression or anxiety too. It's okay if you both need help and support. Don't try to do it on your own."

-Katie, New Mexico, USA

"Find a crew!! Ideally, some new friends that will be going through each stage of motherhood alongside you. It gets super tough always hearing 'it gets easier'. It's wonderful to have a group of women that can say, 'This is really, really hard' and you can share experiences. Not that other friends or other mamas haven't experienced it... but you totally forget what it's like in the thick of it, unless you're actually in it."

-Jamie, Colorado, USA

"…Rest is important for our mental health. When the baby sleeps, take a nap, it is completely okay to let the laundry go until you are down to your last pair of underwear, it is okay to have dishes, and it is okay to sleep. We need sleep, food, water, and also alone time, whether that be when the baby is alone in their crib crying or taking the trash out, a few moments is NECCESSARY. Mental health is important- if you need help, reach out, that is also okay. Many moms are suffering from burnout. Take care of yourself, after all, mental health keeps us going. It is important for you and your baby, I promise you. I have learned the hard way."

-Destany, Colorado, USA

"…Assume that you'll need a therapist or someone neutral to talk to about all the hard stuff. There is hard stuff. Don't let anyone shame you for how you choose to take care of your mental health. Take meds, see a therapist, and make it part of what it means to be a good mom."

-Dylan, North Carolina, USA

"Don't compare yourself to anyone else. Enjoy your baby… it goes by so fast."

-Anonymous, New Mexico, USA

"Take time for yourself, chat to other parents, and don't be too hard on yourself! It's ok to find it hard."

-Kelly, Massachusetts, USA

"Sleep when the baby sleeps, be kind to yourself, not everyone gets it right."

-Kath, Hertfordshire, England

"Talk and listen to people but listen to your gut the most! Be honest about how you feel and don't feel bad when wanting help."

-Nicole, Manchester, England

"It's ok to feel elated, totally in love and happy, the opposite, or all combined. Hormones change a lot- what we feel doesn't define who we are. You've been through a big shift, give yourself grace in however you feel."

-Anonymous, New Mexico, USA

"Take each day at a time. Don't be afraid to ask for help- nobody will judge you. Everything is new to you so don't be too harsh on yourself or have unrealistic expectations. Look after yourself and it will be easier to look after a baby."

-Georgia, Surrey, England

"Attend as many baby classes as possible to make some friends with similar age babies."

-Holly, Manchester, England

"This is harder than you think. You will feel incompetent. You will feel like you need more of you. You are enough."

-Emma, California, USA

"Sleep does wonders. It's really OK to nap while the baby naps."

-Nat, Toronto, Canada

"Don't be afraid to bring up how you're feeling. And don't be afraid to get on meds while pregnant if your doctor advises it."

-Molly, Colorado, USA

"Listen to your inner self and know that it is OK to not be OK. As a new mother you are going through so much change and your hormones are all over the board you are physically and mentally exhausted. Everyone says sleep when the baby sleeps or take me time. That advice is great if you can manage it but so many of us don't have that support system in place. I think the key is to check in with yourself and really try to be honest with yourself about how you were doing and give yourself Grace. It's OK to have hard days and it's OK to have great days. You are not a bad mother if dishes pile up in the sink or if you don't get to the laundry or if you don't use cloth diapers. Everyone has to figure out the challenge on their own terms but I'm going to say again, give yourself Grace and know that it's okay to ask for help. It is a steep learning curve."

-Amy, North Carolina, USA

"…I could not comprehend how I would physically be able to keep meeting the demands of my child like this for the next several months. Every couple hours he needs to eat? I can't sleep more than TWO HOURS in a row for the next several weeks, if not months?! The second time around, I knew better. I knew that it would be hard but that I would survive. I knew it was all worth it and then some. I knew I wasn't alone, that every mother feels this way. Every. Mother. And I knew that, as long as the days felt while I was going through them, when I looked back it would all seem like a blur. The second time, having a newborn still wasn't easy, but I wasn't scared and I cherished as many moments as I could."

-Marisa, Illinois, USA

Chapter 4

On Keeping the Humor

Music to My Ears

*Your giggle floods the room as you push your grocery
cart.*

*I hear your small footsteps running, a sound that fills
my heart.*

*Around and around you go not stopping and no end in
sight.*

*Through your eyes the world is good, everything is
just right.*

*I knew I loved you from the moment I first heard your
heartbeat.*

*From the very top of your head down to your two little
feet.*

*It was hard to imagine those footsteps before you were
here.*

*But now as I watch you run in circles, it's like music
to my ears.*

-Katie Hetman

"Everything you said you weren't going to do-you're gonna do! Every day is a shit show, but if you can laugh about it then it's so much easier! The first week of potty training our son he got a stomach bug and had explosive diarrhea EVERYWHERE! After the fifth time, I just started crying and yelled, I can't take any more shit today! to which my son said, Me either!"

-Kate, New Jersey, USA

"…I know for me personally, on those days I lack the patience sometimes to deal with my 'threenager' the only thing that gets me through a clothing stand-off sometimes is by pretending I'm going to wear his clothing and saying oh this shirt goes on my head right? Essentially it gets his attention and he wants to show me that, no mommy that's not where it goes! So he gets involved and it's involved in a silly way so by the end of it we are both usually laughing."

-Amy, North Carolina, USA

"After our first was born, we were out at a brewery (pre-Covid) feeling like we were nailing this parenting thing when both the umbilical cord plug and the circumcision ring both fell off as my husband was changing him in the bathroom. My husband wrapped it up and came out and gifted it to me because I was sooo ready for those stinky things to come off."

-Anne, Colorado, USA

"...My oldest is now almost 4, and she is hilarious. When covid hit, I was forced to take online classes over zoom. Prior to the start of my class (the day I had a test), I made sure she was watching her show, had her snack, juice, so that she would nap which she normally did, and in the middle of the test, with everyone's microphone on (it was a requirement to have during tests), she screamed, I pooped momma, some people got a giggle out of it, and then she yelled again, in the tub, again my professor and everyone else heard. I immediately got up to see what happened, and low and behold, there was poop.. in the bathtub. She is potty trained, so I asked why she did it. Well, you know that Clorox bleach commercial with the kid pooping in the tub and the mom had to scrub the tub with bleach? Yeah, she had watched that commercial and thought that was a new trend. So, in the middle of the test, I got side-tracked and had to bleach my tub. Life happens- my professor was a mom of 3, thankfully she understood. I finished my test later that night. That's the stuff moms talk about."

-Destany, Colorado, USA

"Have a few kids… the first you have no idea what your doing, the second you do better, the third you might just get it right! Being a mom is the best… being a parent is hard."

-Anonymous, New Mexico, USA

"It's a learning journey! Laugh, cry, share your experience!"

-Kelly, USA

"Record funny sayings or moments on Facebook or an easy place to find on your phone. Just the other day this one popped up on Facebook Memories and I loved being reminded: Me to my daughter 'We are going to the library today!' T-age 3, 'Oh! Books at the library!' Me, 'Yes, books.' T: 'No. Boys at the library!' Lord, help us all!"

-Lauren, Colorado, USA

"Don't take yourself too seriously and laugh when you mess up. It happens to EVERY parent, we make mistakes and learn from them."

-Kara, New Mexico, USA

"My baby was crying in the middle of the night and in the haze of exhaustion and with the lack of light in the room, I picked her up and then screamed as I thought her head had fallen off. It turns out that she was upside down and I was holding her legs! Sounds terrible now but she was fine! And is now a healthy 25-year-old!!"

-Luce

"Poo.... most funny stories with my babies involved exploding nappies and poo.... let's face it babies do a lot of it!! Each of my 5 boys have given me at least 1 extremely memorable and funny poo story...my youngest decided to paint himself, his cot, his bedding and walls with poo....I could hear him in his room laughing and chatting to himself most contently after a morning nap. I went in to get him up only to be confronted with him sitting in the middle of his master piece looking oh so happy with himself....I think if I hadn't laughed I would have cried!"

-Anna

"You need to be able to laugh about some of the stuff that will happen. It isn't easy and won't always be possible, but if you can try to laugh every once in a while, at a diaper explosion covering the walls or the first time your little one drops an F-bomb, you'll be a lot happier and so will they."

-Marisa, Illinois, USA

"When we were anticipating our LO's first laugh, we noticed her glowering at us. We started to worry. Was she constipated? Was she sick? Was she going to be a tiny psychopath?! Her chin tucked, eyebrows knitted, and eyes fixed on us with a menacing stare. Then all of a sudden, she threw her head back and laughed. Cute psychopath."

-Melissa, California, USA

"My daughter came out of our bedroom one day at around age 3 wearing my black bra and my black knee-high boots. She proclaimed what sounded like, 'I'm hot girl!' We were mortified that at the tender age of 3 she has aspirations to be a stripper. We soon figured out when we said, 'you're hot gurl?' that she was saying 'Hawk Girl' a superhero character from a cartoon she was watching!"

-Jennie, Arizona, USA

"Funny faces and noises are the way to bond with your child - they will giggle and wiggle and you will love it."

-Nat, Toronto, Canada

"The sound of your child laughing for the first time…there's nothing like it in the world. Their eyes so joyful and pure, it's worth any stress or heartache. It's in those moments you know you're going to be ok."

-Anonymous, Colorado, USA

"The amazing observations and clever things my two-year-old says. Just yesterday, she sprayed some air freshner in the bathroom after pooping and said, 'I'm making my nose feel better!'"

-Amanda, Colorado, USA

"When my son was first born my husband and I were taking him to my first OB check-up after giving birth. He needed a diaper change while we were waiting for the doctor in the exam room. So using the exam table we began changing him and quickly learned the first rule of baby boys....don't take off the diaper too quickly. He ended up peeing and it went EVERYWHERE. It was the flipping Belaggio Fountains in that room. My husband and I were panic-stricken and trying to contain the pee with our hands, which is the worst thing you could do. We ended up laughing and doing damage control just before the Doctor came in. To keep the humor remember to not sweat the small stuff, there will be accidents and mistakes that's how we all learn, if we can laugh we will create a memory instead of a worry."

-Tiffany, Washington, USA

Chapter 5

On Helpful Items

How Does She Do It?

I see a mom with her kids and can only wonder, how?

How does she do it? One is screaming. What will she
do now?

How does she work and how does she balance life?

She wears so many hats. She is more than a mother
and a wife.

How does she afford the groceries and schedule every
day?

How does she make dinner, clean, and watch the kids
play?

I look down at my belly as I feel him kick back at my
hand.

Feeling unprepared even though this was what I
planned.

I watch the mom kiss each cheek as they load into the
car.

Hoping I can be like that as I watch them from afar.

The mom looks over at me and it's almost like she knew
it.

I hope someday they look at me and wonder how I do it.

-Katie Hetman

"Too many to list all: nose Frida, click connect car seat, pocket bib, Boppy lounger, baby carrier, folding wagon, grovia cloth diapers, wet/dry bag, onesies that zip (not a fan of the all snap outfits), zutano fleece booties."

-Amy, North Carolina, USA

"The advice from our pediatrician which surprised me when I called her in the middle of the night with a sick baby. She said, 'what are your instincts telling you?' She was the expert and yet she was asking me this? She said my instincts were more valuable than I thought and I needed to trust my gut. This was the best thing anyone ever gave me. Her confidence in me made me a better mom."

-Lauren, Colorado, USA

"A child wearing device, a great chair to rock and sleep in, bath visor to keep water out of littles eyes."

-Kate, New Jersey, USA

"Don't buy a diaper bag! There isn't anything special about them. Just use a bag you like. Really you need a way to get baby from point A-B, a plan for feeding, a plan for the poop & pee, a place for baby to sleep, and some clothes. Don't buy too much because you will have stuff you don't need and won't have the stuff that you do need."

-Dylan, North Carolina, USA

"Nipple covers that caught milk and could go in the freezer."

-Kath, Herefordshire, UK

"The Frida nose sucker, Chux from the hospital for blow-out diaper changes, Johnson & Johnson nighttime lotion, sleep sacks, and the nursing bras from target that are mega comfortable to sleep in."

-Kara, New Mexico, USA

"Comfy pillows, clothes, oils, and herbal teas."

-Nicole, Manchester, UK

"Lots of dummies, tons of baby bottles, bibs, muslin squares, packs of wipes, teething rings or toys, sleeping bags for baby to sleep in, baby carrier, the essentials, playpen or bouncer to keep baby occupied while doing quick tasks baby-free."

-Georgia, Surrey, UK

"Those velcro baby swaddlers. The winter bunting that covers the strollers (for city moms like I was). Lots and lots of footed pajamas. Boobs. Breastfeeding isn't for everyone, but let me tell you--not having to wash bottles and nipples, and not having to heat up a bottle in the middle of the night, or pack a bottle when going out, was so great."

-Marisa, Illinois, USA

"Bathrobes that make me feel sexy."

-Emma, California, USA

"As a new mother to be most are eager to go out and buy the trendy expensive gadgets that they tell us that we can't live without but seriously a baby really doesn't care if it's a $100 pram or a $1000 pram! The thing that I would invest the most research and money into is the car seat. The thing that my babies loved the most and I used through all 5 children was a jolly jumper with an A-frame stand and interactive floor mat!"

-Anna

"Diaper pads for overnights, you will get more sleep! A tub of Vaseline and a spatula instead of expensive diaper cream, their college fund will thank you. A floor bed and fully baby-proofed room will get you a few extra minutes of sleep while they play. A magnetic CPR diagram in the kitchen, you never know when you might need it. Infant pain reliever/fever reducer, when you need it you NEED it you won't have time to go out and get it—travel with it. Everything else is extra."

-Melissa, California, USA

"You can live without items, you can't live without a support system."

-Naba, Canada

"It really changes with each child. A baby sling is very helpful these days and much more comfortable than the old Baby Bjorne carriers. Nursing pads are a must. Bubble bath for you."

-Jennie, Arizona, USA

"A carrier. Babies always want to be close so to be able to walk around hands-free with baby and get stuff done was a necessity! Also worked beautifully when taking baby grocery shopping or playdates for older siblings."

-Tiffany, Washington, USA

Chapter 6

On Resources

Grandpa in Heaven

Grandma says I have your eyes, your stride, and your feet.
I can feel you here with me even though we never got to meet.
I imagine a day with you here where we run, jump, and laugh.
The memories we never got to make. Adventures we would never have.
Mommy says you love me and you're somewhere up above.
She points to my heart. Says close my eyes and I can feel your love.
I see your picture on the wall and feel a sense of pride.
But I long to hear your voice and wish you were by my side.
-Katie Hetman

We have listed helpful resources for mothers below, from breastfeeding, mental health to adoption support. We are not sponsored by any of these organizations but feel they can be helpful, regardless of where you are in your motherhood journey.

MOPS

From their website: Here at MOPS, we gather and support moms. We believe in the simple but revolutionary idea that remarkable things happen when moms come together.

Website: https://www.mops.org/

Act for Youth

From their website: The MIECHV Program supports home visits for pregnant women and parents living in vulnerable communities.

Website: https://actforyouth.net/

La Leche League

From their website: La Leche League International is a worldwide educational, non-sectarian, not-for-profit, volunteer-based organization. We provide breastfeeding information and support to those who want to breastfeed their infants.

Website: https://www.llli.org/

Postpartum Support International

From their website: Our purpose is to increase awareness among public and professional communities about the emotional changes that women experience during pregnancy and postpartum.

Website: www.postpartum.net/

Or text: "help" to 800-944-4773 (English)

Or 971-203-7773 (Español)

Dona International

From their website: DONA International is the leader in evidence-based doula training, certification, and continuing education.

Website: https://www.dona.org/

Embrace Families

From their website: Embrace Families provides resources, guidance, and counseling to families following their adoption.

Website: https://embracefamilies.org/find-support/adoptive-parents

March of Dimes

From their website: Hundreds of thousands of families all across the country are impacted by preterm birth, a NICU stay, or loss. Find a supportive online environment that's just right for you with trusted information and advice, helpful resources, and caring people who want to connect.

Website: www.marchofdimes.org

Circle of Parents

From their website: Circle of Parents groups meet weekly, are free of charge, and foster an open exchange of ideas, support, information, and resources. These kinds of groups serve those parenting children of all ages and families of all types.

Website: http://circleofparents.org/

When asked to describe motherhood in one word, this is what our mothers said:

Afterword

It's incredible. One day your house is filled with sippy cups, wipes and crayons, the ground full of foot dynamite waiting to be stepped on. It's the most beautiful mayhem. In that moment, time rushes, catching up…you're not in college waiting on an exam score. You're not speeding home from work at 9 p.m. to get ready to drink with friends. You suddenly understand the life you've created, the most miraculous of designs. The singing, the dirt, the love. It's what everything else was waiting for, this moment.

We hope you take a minute, a breath. When days seem hard, you're not alone. It's ok to cry, it's ok to set Google aside and listen to your instinct as a mother. It's ok to go against the grain if it feels right in your heart. Trust yourself. You're enough.

We hope this guide was helpful, and that you pass it along to others ready to start their own motherhood journey.

About the Authors

Amanda Smith is the mother of two spunky daughters and author of novels *Year 2160* and *Paper and Ink.* She has a master's degree in clinical social work and currently works for a hospice. Amanda writes both essays, short stories and works of fiction for her blog, *In the Wright.* She is a lifelong learner and lover of space, happy debates among friends, and hiking through the Colorado wilderness.

Katie Hetman is a mother of two adventurous sons with a third baby on the way. She recently left her 10-year career in accounting to be a stay-at-home mom at the start of the COVID-19 pandemic. She enjoys writing poetry, uplifting others, and of course, being a mom. Poetry has been the bridge between her and the mom community to empower, encourage, and bring together moms everywhere.